INSULIN RESISTANCE DIET
FOR BEGINNERS

Dr. Mary Williams

Disclaimer

Please keep in mind that the content in this book is solely for educational purposes. The information offered here is said to be reliable and trustworthy. The author makes no implication or intends to offer any warranty of accuracy for particular individual cases.

Before beginning any diet or lifestyle habits, it is recommended that you contact a knowledgeable practitioner, such as your doctor. This book's material should not be utilized in place of expert counsel or professional guidance.

The author, publisher, and distributor expressly disclaim all liability, loss, damage, or danger incurred by persons who rely on the information in this book, whether directly or indirectly.

All intellectual property rights are retained. This book's information should not be replicated in any way, mechanically, electronically, photocopying, or by any other methods accessible

TABLE OF CONTENTS

WHY THIS IS NOT YOUR EVERYDAY BOOK

In a world filled with culinary temptations and an ever-growing list of dietary options, finding a path to health can often feel like navigating a maze in the dark. For those battling insulin resistance, the journey can be particularly challenging, as it demands a delicate balance between indulgence and nutritional wisdom. But fear not, for you now hold in your hands a beacon of hope—a culinary compass to guide you through the intricacies of managing insulin resistance with ease, flavor, and boundless joy.

This is not just a cookbook; it is a passport to a world where your health and happiness are seamlessly intertwined. Imagine a world where every bite you take is not only a celebration of flavor but also a step towards mastering your body's response to insulin. This isn't just another cookbook; it's your culinary ally on the journey to wellness.

Here, we offer you a treasure trove of 60 delectable recipes meticulously crafted to delight your taste buds while nurturing your health. Our culinary creations are thoughtfully categorized into three sections, ensuring that every meal of the day becomes a chance to nourish your body and soul:

Morning Delights: Start your day with a symphony of flavors that harmonize with your health goals. From Cinnamon Apple Oatmeal Bowls that warm your soul to Sweet Potato and Turkey Hash that invigorates your senses, our breakfast recipes are designed to kickstart your day on the right foot.

Lunchtime Euphoria: Lunches are more than mere sustenance; they are moments of rejuvenation. Dive into our Spinach and Mushroom Breakfast Quesadilla or Mediterranean Baked Cod, and experience the joy of a midday meal that fuels your body without compromising on taste.

Dinner Serenades: Your evenings are reserved for culinary crescendos that soothe and satisfy. Whether you're savoring a Baked Sweet Potato with Black Bean Chili or a Lemon Dill Grilled Swordfish, our dinner recipes promise a sensory experience that transforms your dining table into a stage for culinary artistry.

But what sets this cookbook apart from the rest?

Nutritional Wisdom Meets Culinary Artistry: Every recipe in this book has been carefully curated to include ingredients that align with insulin resistance management. You'll find a harmonious blend of whole grains, lean proteins, healthy fats, and fiber-rich produce, all expertly combined to keep your blood sugar levels steady while sating your cravings.

Flavors from Around the World: Embark on a global gastronomic journey as we bring you tastes and techniques from various cuisines. From Thai Red Curry with Tofu to Ratatouille Stuffed Bell Peppers, your palate will dance across continents, savoring an array of exciting flavors, and so much more.

Easy-to-Follow, Inspiring Instructions: We understand that the kitchen can be an intimidating place. That's why each recipe is accompanied by clear, step-by-step instructions and tips to empower even the novice chef. We encourage you to embrace the joy of cooking and the empowerment of knowing exactly what goes onto your plate.

A Lifestyle, Not a Diet: We believe in sustainable choices and long-term well-being. This book isn't about restriction; it's about mindful choices that become second nature. Our recipes embrace balance, so you can enjoy life's culinary pleasures without compromising your health. And so much more.

So, dear reader, as you embark on this culinary voyage with us, remember that you're not just holding a cookbook; you're holding the key to a life where insulin resistance is managed with grace, where your taste buds rejoice, and where you rediscover the joy of nourishing your body and soul.

Welcome to a world where harmony truly resides on your plate. The journey starts now, and we're thrilled to have you as our companion.

Bon appétit, and may your journey to insulin resistance management be filled with health, happiness, and delicious discoveries!

RECIPES

Cinnamon Apple Oatmeal Bowl

Intro: Start your day with a comforting and nutritious Cinnamon Apple Oatmeal Bowl. This recipe is rich in fiber and complex carbohydrates, making it an excellent choice for managing insulin resistance.
Total Time: 15 minutes

Ingredients:
- 1/2 cup rolled oats
- 1 cup unsweetened almond milk
- 1/2 teaspoon ground cinnamon
- 1 small apple, diced
- 1 tablespoon chopped walnuts
- 1 teaspoon honey (optional)

Directions:
1. In a small saucepan, combine rolled oats and almond milk. Bring to a gentle boil over medium heat, then reduce heat to low and simmer for about 5 minutes, stirring occasionally.
2. Stir in the ground cinnamon and diced apple. Continue to cook for an additional 2-3 minutes until the apples soften.
3. Transfer the oatmeal to a bowl and top it with chopped walnuts. Drizzle with honey if desired.
4. Serve hot and enjoy your Cinnamon Apple Oatmeal Bowl!

Nutritional Information:
- Calories: 320
- Carbohydrates: 54g
- Protein: 7g
- Fat: 10g
- Fiber: 9g
- Sugar: 17g

Spinach and Feta Breakfast Wrap

Intro: This Spinach and Feta Breakfast Wrap is a quick and easy morning meal that's packed with protein and greens to help stabilize blood sugar levels.

Total Time: 15 minutes

Ingredients:
- 2 whole wheat tortillas
- 4 large eggs, beaten
- 1 cup fresh spinach leaves
- 1/4 cup crumbled feta cheese
- Salt and pepper to taste
- Cooking spray

Directions:
1. In a non-stick skillet, heat cooking spray over medium heat. Add beaten eggs, spinach, and a pinch of salt and pepper. Cook, stirring occasionally, until the eggs are set and the spinach wilts, about 3-4 minutes.
2. Warm the whole wheat tortillas in a dry skillet or microwave for about 10 seconds.
3. Divide the scrambled egg and spinach mixture evenly between the two tortillas. Sprinkle each with crumbled feta cheese.
4. Roll up the tortillas, tucking in the sides as you go, to create wraps.
5. Serve hot, and enjoy your Spinach and Feta Breakfast Wrap!

Nutritional Information:
- Calories: 320
- Carbohydrates: 24g
- Protein: 18g
- Fat: 18g
- Fiber: 3g
- Sugar: 2g

Blueberry Almond Pancakes

Intro: These Blueberry Almond Pancakes are a delightful way to start your day. They're low in added sugar and rich in fiber and antioxidants, thanks to the blueberries.

Total Time: 25 minutes

Ingredients:
- 1 cup whole wheat flour
- 2 tablespoons almond meal
- 1 teaspoon baking powder
- 1/2 teaspoon baking soda
- 1/4 teaspoon salt
- 1 cup unsweetened almond milk
- 1 large egg
- 1 tablespoon maple syrup
- 1/2 teaspoon almond extract
- 1/2 cup fresh blueberries
- Cooking spray

Directions:
1. In a large mixing bowl, whisk together the whole wheat flour, almond meal, baking powder, baking soda, and salt.
2. In a separate bowl, whisk together the almond milk, egg, maple syrup, and almond extract.
3. Pour the wet ingredients into the dry ingredients and stir until just combined. Gently fold in the blueberries.
4. Heat a non-stick skillet or griddle over medium heat and lightly grease with cooking spray.
5. Pour 1/4 cup of the pancake batter onto the skillet for each pancake. Cook until bubbles form on the surface, then flip and cook the other side until golden brown.
6. Serve hot with additional blueberries and a drizzle of maple syrup if desired.
7. Enjoy your Blueberry Almond Pancakes!

Nutritional Information:
- Calories: 250
- Carbohydrates: 38g
- Protein: 7g
- Fat: 7g
- Fiber: 5g

- Sugar: 6g

Veggie Omelette Delight

Intro: This Veggie Omelette Delight is a nutrient-packed breakfast that's low in carbohydrates and high in protein. It's perfect for maintaining stable blood sugar levels.

Total Time: 15 minutes

Ingredients:
- 2 large eggs
- 2 egg whites
- 1/4 cup diced bell peppers (any color)
- 1/4 cup diced tomatoes
- 1/4 cup diced onions
- 1/4 cup sliced mushrooms
- 1/4 cup spinach leaves
- Salt and pepper to taste
- Cooking spray

Directions:
1. In a bowl, whisk together the eggs and egg whites. Season with a pinch of salt and pepper.
2. Heat a non-stick skillet over medium heat and coat it with cooking spray.
3. Add the diced bell peppers, tomatoes, onions, and mushrooms to the skillet. Sauté for about 3-4 minutes until the vegetables start to soften.
4. Pour the whisked eggs over the sautéed vegetables and cook, without stirring, for about 2-3 minutes, until the edges set.
5. Carefully lift the edges of the omelette with a spatula to allow any uncooked eggs to flow to the bottom.
6. Add the spinach leaves on one half of the omelette and fold the other half over the top.
7. Continue cooking for another 1-2 minutes until the omelette is fully cooked but still moist inside.
8. Slide the Veggie Omelette Delight onto a plate, cut it in half, and serve hot.
9. Enjoy your Veggie Omelette Delight!

Nutritional Information:
- Calories: 180
- Carbohydrates: 9g
- Protein: 20g
- Fat: 8g
- Fiber: 3g
- Sugar: 3g

Chia Seed Pudding with Berries

Intro: Chia Seed Pudding with Berries is a nutritious and filling breakfast that's rich in omega-3 fatty acids and antioxidants. It's a perfect choice for managing insulin resistance.

Total Time: 4 hours (includes chilling time)

Ingredients:
- 1/4 cup chia seeds
- 1 cup unsweetened almond milk
- 1/2 teaspoon vanilla extract
- 1 tablespoon maple syrup
- 1/2 cup mixed berries (strawberries, blueberries, raspberries)
- 1 tablespoon chopped nuts (e.g., almonds, walnuts)

Directions:
1. In a bowl, whisk together the chia seeds, almond milk, vanilla extract, and maple syrup.
2. Cover the bowl and refrigerate for at least 4 hours or overnight to allow the chia seeds to absorb the liquid and create a pudding-like consistency.
3. Before serving, give the chia pudding a good stir to evenly distribute the seeds.
4. Serve the pudding in individual bowls or jars, topped with mixed berries and chopped nuts.
5. Enjoy your Chia Seed Pudding with Berries!

Nutritional Information:
- Calories: 220
- Carbohydrates: 24g

- Protein: 6g
- Fat: 11g
- Fiber: 10g
- Sugar: 8g

Sweet Potato and Turkey Hash

Intro: Sweet Potato and Turkey Hash is a hearty and satisfying breakfast that's low in processed carbohydrates and packed with protein. It's an ideal choice for managing insulin resistance.

Total Time: 25 minutes

Ingredients:
- 1 large sweet potato, peeled and diced
- 1/2 pound ground turkey
- 1/2 cup diced bell peppers (any color)
- 1/4 cup diced onions
- 1/2 teaspoon smoked paprika
- 1/4 teaspoon garlic powder
- Salt and pepper to taste
- Cooking spray
- Chopped fresh parsley for garnish (optional)

Directions:
1. In a large skillet, heat cooking spray over medium-high heat. Add the diced sweet potato and cook, stirring occasionally, until they are tender and slightly crispy, about 10-12 minutes.
2. Push the sweet potatoes to one side of the skillet and add the ground turkey to the other side. Cook the turkey, breaking it apart with a spatula, until it's browned and cooked through, about 5-7 minutes.
3. Stir in the diced bell peppers and onions, and cook for an additional 3-4 minutes until they soften.
4. Season the entire mixture with smoked paprika, garlic powder, salt, and pepper. Stir to combine.
5. Serve hot, garnished with chopped fresh parsley if desired.
6. Enjoy your Sweet Potato and Turkey Hash!

Nutritional Information:
- Calories: 300
- Carbohydrates: 30g
- Protein: 20g
- Fat: 12g
- Fiber: 5g
- Sugar: 7g

Greek Yogurt Parfait with Nuts and Honey

Intro: This Greek Yogurt Parfait with Nuts and Honey is a protein-packed breakfast that's low in added sugars. It's perfect for maintaining stable blood sugar levels.

Total Time: 5 minutes

Ingredients:
- 1 cup plain Greek yogurt
- 1/4 cup mixed nuts (almonds, walnuts, and pecans)
- 1 tablespoon honey
- 1/2 cup fresh mixed berries (strawberries, blueberries, raspberries)

Directions:
1. In a serving bowl or glass, start with a layer of Greek yogurt.
2. Add a layer of mixed nuts on top of the yogurt.
3. Drizzle honey over the nuts.
4. Add a layer of fresh mixed berries.
5. Repeat the layers as desired, finishing with a drizzle of honey on top.
6. Serve immediately, and enjoy your Greek Yogurt Parfait with Nuts and Honey!

Nutritional Information:
- Calories: 320
- Carbohydrates: 29g
- Protein: 16g
- Fat: 18g
- Fiber: 4g
- Sugar: 17g

Quinoa Breakfast Bowl

Intro: Start your day with a protein-packed Quinoa Breakfast Bowl filled with fresh ingredients. This breakfast is low in processed sugars and high in fiber.
Total Time: 20 minutes

Ingredients:
- 1 cup cooked quinoa
- 1/2 cup unsweetened almond milk
- 1 tablespoon almond butter
- 1/2 banana, sliced
- 1/4 cup fresh mixed berries (strawberries, blueberries, raspberries)
- 1 tablespoon chopped nuts (e.g., almonds, walnuts)
- 1/2 teaspoon cinnamon
- 1 teaspoon honey (optional)

Directions:
1. In a bowl, combine the cooked quinoa and almond milk. Stir in the almond butter and mix until well combined.
2. Top the quinoa mixture with sliced banana, mixed berries, chopped nuts, and a sprinkle of cinnamon.
3. Drizzle with honey if desired.
4. Serve warm, and enjoy your Quinoa Breakfast Bowl!

Nutritional Information:
- Calories: 350
- Carbohydrates: 53g
- Protein: 9g
- Fat: 11g
- Fiber: 7g
- Sugar: 10g

Avocado and Egg Breakfast Tacos

Intro: These Avocado and Egg Breakfast Tacos are a delicious way to start your day with healthy fats and protein. They are perfect for managing insulin resistance.

Total Time: 15 minutes

Ingredients:
- 2 small whole wheat tortillas
- 2 large eggs
- 1 ripe avocado, sliced
- 1/4 cup diced tomatoes
- 1/4 cup diced onions
- 1/4 cup fresh cilantro leaves
- Salt and pepper to taste
- Cooking spray

Directions:
1. Heat a non-stick skillet over medium heat and coat it with cooking spray.
2. In a bowl, whisk the eggs and season with a pinch of salt and pepper.
3. Pour the whisked eggs into the skillet and cook, stirring occasionally, until they are scrambled and cooked to your liking, about 3-4 minutes.
4. Warm the whole wheat tortillas in a dry skillet or microwave for about 10 seconds.
5. Divide the scrambled eggs between the two tortillas.
6. Top each taco with sliced avocado, diced tomatoes, diced onions, and fresh cilantro leaves.
7. Serve hot, and enjoy your Avocado and Egg Breakfast Tacos!

Nutritional Information:
- Calories: 350
- Carbohydrates: 30g
- Protein: 13g
- Fat: 22g
- Fiber: 9g
- Sugar: 4g

Banana Nut Whole Wheat Muffins

Intro: These Banana Nut Whole Wheat Muffins are a wholesome and tasty breakfast option that's low in added sugars and high in fiber. They are perfect for managing insulin resistance.

Total Time: 30 minutes

Ingredients:
- 1 1/2 cups whole wheat flour
- 1/2 cup rolled oats
- 1/4 cup chopped walnuts
- 1 teaspoon baking powder
- 1/2 teaspoon baking soda
- 1/4 teaspoon salt
- 2 ripe bananas, mashed
- 1/4 cup honey
- 1/4 cup unsweetened applesauce
- 1/4 cup plain Greek yogurt
- 1 large egg
- 1 teaspoon vanilla extract

Directions:
1. Preheat your oven to 350°F (175°C). Line a muffin tin with paper liners or grease the cups with cooking spray.
2. In a large mixing bowl, combine the whole wheat flour, rolled oats, chopped walnuts, baking powder, baking soda, and salt.
3. In another bowl, mash the ripe bananas and stir in the honey, unsweetened applesauce, plain Greek yogurt, egg, and vanilla extract.
4. Pour the wet ingredients into the dry ingredients and stir until just combined.
5. Divide the batter evenly among the muffin cups.
6. Bake for 18-20 minutes or until a toothpick inserted into the center of a muffin comes out clean.
7. Allow the muffins to cool in the pan for a few minutes, then transfer them to a wire rack to cool completely.
8. Enjoy your Banana Nut Whole Wheat Muffins!

Nutritional Information (per muffin):
- Calories: 160
- Carbohydrates: 32g
- Protein: 4g
- Fat: 3g

- Fiber: 4g
- Sugar: 12g

Spinach and Mushroom Breakfast Quesadilla

Intro: Start your day with a flavorful and protein-packed Spinach and Mushroom Breakfast Quesadilla. It's a delicious way to incorporate greens into your morning routine.

Total Time: 20 minutes

Ingredients:
- 2 whole wheat tortillas
- 2 large eggs
- 1 cup fresh spinach leaves
- 1/2 cup sliced mushrooms
- 1/4 cup shredded cheddar cheese
- Salt and pepper to taste
- Cooking spray

Directions:
1. Heat a non-stick skillet over medium heat and coat it with cooking spray.
2. In a bowl, whisk the eggs and season with a pinch of salt and pepper.
3. Pour the whisked eggs into the skillet and cook, stirring occasionally, until they are scrambled and cooked to your liking, about 3-4 minutes.
4. Remove the scrambled eggs from the skillet and set them aside.
5. In the same skillet, add a bit more cooking spray and sauté the sliced mushrooms until they become tender, about 3-4 minutes.
6. Place one whole wheat tortilla in the skillet. Sprinkle half of the shredded cheddar cheese evenly on the tortilla.
7. Add half of the scrambled eggs on top of the cheese, followed by half of the sautéed mushrooms and fresh spinach leaves.
8. Place the second tortilla on top and press gently.
9. Cook for about 2-3 minutes on each side until the quesadilla is heated through and the cheese is melted.
10. Remove from the skillet, cut into wedges, and serve hot.
11. Enjoy your Spinach and Mushroom Breakfast Quesadilla!

Nutritional Information:
- Calories: 340
- Carbohydrates: 29g
- Protein: 20g
- Fat: 16g
- Fiber: 6g
- Sugar: 2g

Overnight Oats with Almonds and Berries

Intro: These Overnight Oats with Almonds and Berries are a convenient and nutritious breakfast option that can be prepared in advance. They are rich in fiber and antioxidants.
Total Time: 5 minutes (plus overnight chilling)

Ingredients:
- 1/2 cup rolled oats
- 1 cup unsweetened almond milk
- 2 tablespoons chopped almonds
- 1/2 cup mixed berries (strawberries, blueberries, raspberries)
- 1 tablespoon honey (optional)

Directions:
1. In a mason jar or airtight container, combine the rolled oats and unsweetened almond milk.
2. Stir in the chopped almonds and mixed berries.
3. If desired, drizzle with honey.
4. Cover the container and refrigerate overnight (or for at least 4 hours) to allow the oats to soak and thicken.
5. In the morning, give the oats a good stir before serving.
6. Enjoy your Overnight Oats with Almonds and Berries!

Nutritional Information:
- Calories: 280
- Carbohydrates: 42g
- Protein: 7g
- Fat: 9g

- Fiber: 7g
- Sugar: 10g

Smoked Salmon and Cream Cheese Toast

Intro: Indulge in a gourmet breakfast with this Smoked Salmon and Cream Cheese Toast. It's a delightful combination of flavors and textures that's perfect for a special morning.

Total Time: 10 minutes

Ingredients:
- 2 slices whole grain bread, toasted
- 2 tablespoons low-fat cream cheese
- 2 ounces smoked salmon
- 1 tablespoon capers
- Fresh dill for garnish (optional)
- Lemon wedges for serving (optional)

Directions:
1. Spread a tablespoon of low-fat cream cheese on each slice of toasted whole grain bread.
2. Arrange the smoked salmon on top of the cream cheese.
3. Sprinkle capers over the smoked salmon.
4. Garnish with fresh dill if desired.
5. Serve with lemon wedges on the side for an extra burst of flavor.
6. Enjoy your Smoked Salmon and Cream Cheese Toast!

Nutritional Information:
- Calories: 280
- Carbohydrates: 29g
- Protein: 20g
- Fat: 9g
- Fiber: 6g
- Sugar: 4g

Pumpkin Spice Smoothie

Intro: This Pumpkin Spice Smoothie is a seasonal delight that's perfect for fall mornings. It's a low-sugar, high-fiber breakfast option with the warm flavors of autumn.

Total Time: 5 minutes

Ingredients:
- 1/2 cup canned pumpkin puree
- 1/2 cup unsweetened almond milk
- 1/2 banana
- 1/4 cup Greek yogurt
- 1/2 teaspoon pumpkin spice
- 1 tablespoon honey (optional)
- Ice cubes (optional)

Directions:
1. In a blender, combine the canned pumpkin puree, unsweetened almond milk, banana, Greek yogurt, and pumpkin spice.
2. If you desire added sweetness, add a tablespoon of honey.
3. Optionally, add a few ice cubes to make the smoothie cold.
4. Blend until smooth and creamy.
5. Pour into a glass and sprinkle with additional pumpkin spice for garnish if desired.
6. Enjoy your Pumpkin Spice Smoothie!

Nutritional Information:
- Calories: 210
- Carbohydrates: 40g
- Protein: 7g
- Fat: 4g
- Fiber: 7g
- Sugar: 18g

Mediterranean Breakfast Bowl

Intro: Transport your taste buds to the Mediterranean with this flavorful and nutritious Mediterranean Breakfast Bowl. It's a balanced breakfast option that's perfect for managing insulin resistance.

Total Time: 15 minutes

Ingredients:
- 1/2 cup cooked quinoa
- 1/4 cup hummus
- 1/4 cup diced cucumbers
- 1/4 cup diced tomatoes
- 2 tablespoons chopped kalamata olives
- 2 tablespoons crumbled feta cheese
- Fresh parsley for garnish (optional)
- Olive oil drizzle (optional)

Directions:
1. In a bowl, start with a layer of cooked quinoa.
2. Add a dollop of hummus on top of the quinoa.
3. Sprinkle diced cucumbers, diced tomatoes, kalamata olives, and crumbled feta cheese evenly over the hummus.
4. Garnish with fresh parsley if desired and drizzle with a bit of olive oil.
5. Enjoy your Mediterranean Breakfast Bowl!

Nutritional Information:
- Calories: 320
- Carbohydrates: 30g
- Protein: 9g
- Fat: 19g
- Fiber: 6g
- Sugar: 3g

Zucchini and Mushroom Frittata

Intro: This Zucchini and Mushroom Frittata is a savory breakfast option packed with vegetables and protein. It's a great choice for managing insulin resistance.

Total Time: 25 minutes

Ingredients:
- 6 large eggs
- 1 medium zucchini, thinly sliced
- 1 cup sliced mushrooms
- 1/2 cup diced onions
- 1/4 cup grated Parmesan cheese
- 1 tablespoon olive oil
- Salt and pepper to taste
- Fresh basil for garnish (optional)

Directions:
1. Preheat your oven's broiler.
2. In a large ovenproof skillet, heat olive oil over medium heat. Add diced onions and sauté until they become translucent, about 2-3 minutes.
3. Add the sliced zucchini and mushrooms to the skillet. Cook, stirring occasionally, until they soften, about 5 minutes.
4. In a bowl, whisk together the eggs and grated Parmesan cheese. Season with a pinch of salt and pepper.
5. Pour the egg mixture evenly over the sautéed vegetables in the skillet.
6. Cook on the stovetop for 3-4 minutes, or until the edges of the frittata begin to set.
7. Transfer the skillet to the preheated broiler and broil for about 2-3 minutes, until the top is golden brown and the frittata is set in the center.
8. Carefully remove the skillet from the oven (using oven mitts), and let it cool slightly.
9. Garnish with fresh basil if desired.
10. Slice and serve your Zucchini and Mushroom Frittata.
11. Enjoy!

Nutritional Information:
- Calories: 190
- Carbohydrates: 6g
- Protein: 13g
- Fat: 13g
- Fiber: 2g
- Sugar: 3g

Almond Butter and Banana Sandwich

Intro: The Almond Butter and Banana Sandwich is a simple yet satisfying breakfast option. It provides healthy fats, protein, and natural sweetness for managing insulin resistance.
Total Time: 5 minutes

Ingredients:
- 2 slices whole grain bread, toasted
- 2 tablespoons almond butter
- 1 ripe banana, sliced
- 1 teaspoon honey (optional)

Directions:
1. Spread a tablespoon of almond butter on each slice of toasted whole grain bread.
2. Arrange the sliced banana on one of the slices.
3. If desired, drizzle with honey for added sweetness.
4. Place the second slice of bread on top to create a sandwich.
5. Cut in half diagonally if preferred.
6. Enjoy your Almond Butter and Banana Sandwich!

Nutritional Information:
- Calories: 320
- Carbohydrates: 47g
- Protein: 7g
- Fat: 14g
- Fiber: 7g
- Sugar: 18g

Breakfast Burrito with Black Beans

Intro: This Breakfast Burrito with Black Beans is a protein-packed way to start your day. It's loaded with fiber and flavor, making it a great choice for managing insulin resistance.
Total Time: 20 minutes

Ingredients:

- 2 whole wheat tortillas
- 4 large eggs, beaten
- 1/2 cup canned black beans, drained and rinsed
- 1/4 cup diced onions
- 1/4 cup diced bell peppers (any color)
- 1/4 cup shredded cheddar cheese
- Salt and pepper to taste
- Cooking spray
- Fresh salsa for topping (optional)

Directions:

1. Heat a non-stick skillet over medium heat and coat it with cooking spray.
2. Add diced onions and diced bell peppers to the skillet. Sauté for about 3-4 minutes until they start to soften.
3. Add beaten eggs and cook, stirring occasionally, until they are scrambled and cooked to your liking, about 3-4 minutes.
4. Warm the whole wheat tortillas in a dry skillet or microwave for about 10 seconds.
5. Divide the scrambled egg mixture evenly between the two tortillas.
6. Sprinkle black beans and shredded cheddar cheese on top of the eggs.
7. Roll up the tortillas, tucking in the sides as you go, to create burritos.
8. Serve hot with fresh salsa if desired.
9. Enjoy your Breakfast Burrito with Black Beans!

Nutritional Information:

- Calories: 350
- Carbohydrates: 30g
- Protein: 20g
- Fat: 17g
- Fiber: 7g
- Sugar: 3g

Coconut Chia Seed Smoothie

Intro: This Coconut Chia Seed Smoothie is a creamy and nutritious breakfast option rich in fiber and healthy fats. It's a great choice for managing insulin resistance.

Total Time: 5 minutes

Ingredients:
- 1 cup unsweetened coconut milk
- 2 tablespoons chia seeds
- 1/2 banana
- 1/2 cup frozen pineapple chunks
- 1 tablespoon honey (optional)

Directions:
1. In a blender, combine unsweetened coconut milk and chia seeds. Let the mixture sit for 5-10 minutes to allow the chia seeds to absorb some of the liquid.
2. Add the banana and frozen pineapple chunks to the blender.
3. If desired, add a tablespoon of honey for sweetness.
4. Blend until smooth and creamy.
5. Pour into a glass and enjoy your Coconut Chia Seed Smoothie!

Nutritional Information:
- Calories: 280
- Carbohydrates: 38g
- Protein: 4g
- Fat: 14g
- Fiber: 8g
- Sugar: 20g

Tomato and Basil Breakfast Bruschetta

Intro: This Tomato and Basil Breakfast Bruschetta is a fresh and flavorful way to start your day. It's a low-sugar, high-fiber breakfast option that's perfect for managing insulin resistance.

Total Time: 15 minutes

Ingredients:
- 4 slices whole grain baguette, toasted
- 2 large tomatoes, diced
- 1/4 cup fresh basil leaves, chopped
- 1 clove garlic, minced
- 1 tablespoon balsamic vinegar
- 1 tablespoon olive oil
- Salt and pepper to taste
- 4 poached or fried eggs (optional)

Directions:
1. In a bowl, combine the diced tomatoes, chopped fresh basil, minced garlic, balsamic vinegar, and olive oil. Season with salt and pepper. Mix well.
2. Toast the slices of whole grain baguette until they are lightly crispy.
3. Spoon the tomato and basil mixture onto each toasted baguette slice.
4. If desired, top each bruschetta with a poached or fried egg.
5. Serve immediately and enjoy your Tomato and Basil Breakfast Bruschetta!

Nutritional Information (per bruschetta without eggs):
- Calories: 90
- Carbohydrates: 15g
- Protein: 3g
- Fat: 3g
- Fiber: 2g
- Sugar: 3g

Grilled Chicken and Avocado Salad

Intro: Enjoy a delicious and nutritious Grilled Chicken and Avocado Salad that's packed with protein and healthy fats. It's a perfect meal for managing insulin resistance.
Total Time: 25 minutes

Ingredients:
- 2 boneless, skinless chicken breasts
- 2 teaspoons olive oil
- Salt and pepper to taste

- 4 cups mixed greens (e.g., spinach, arugula, romaine)
- 1 ripe avocado, sliced
- 1 cup cherry tomatoes, halved
- 1/4 red onion, thinly sliced
- 2 tablespoons balsamic vinaigrette dressing

Directions:

1. Preheat your grill or grill pan to medium-high heat.
2. Brush the chicken breasts with olive oil and season with salt and pepper.
3. Grill the chicken for about 6-7 minutes per side, or until it's cooked through and has grill marks. The internal temperature should reach 165°F (74°C).
4. Remove the chicken from the grill, let it rest for a few minutes, then slice it into thin strips.
5. In a large salad bowl, arrange the mixed greens.
6. Top the greens with sliced avocado, cherry tomatoes, and thinly sliced red onion.
7. Add the grilled chicken on top.
8. Drizzle the salad with balsamic vinaigrette dressing.
9. Toss the salad gently to combine all the ingredients.
10. Serve immediately and enjoy your Grilled Chicken and Avocado Salad!

Nutritional Information:
- Calories: 350
- Carbohydrates: 15g
- Protein: 30g
- Fat: 20g
- Fiber: 6g
- Sugar: 4g

Lentil and Spinach Soup

Intro: Warm up with a hearty Lentil and Spinach Soup that's rich in fiber and plant-based protein. It's a great choice for managing insulin resistance.
Total Time: 40 minutes

Ingredients:
- 1 cup dry green or brown lentils, rinsed and drained
- 1 onion, chopped
- 2 carrots, peeled and diced
- 2 celery stalks, diced
- 3 cloves garlic, minced
- 6 cups vegetable broth
- 1 teaspoon ground cumin
- 1/2 teaspoon ground coriander
- 1/2 teaspoon smoked paprika
- Salt and pepper to taste
- 4 cups fresh spinach leaves
- Juice of 1 lemon
- Fresh parsley for garnish (optional)

Directions:
1. In a large soup pot, heat a bit of vegetable broth over medium heat. Add chopped onion, carrots, celery, and garlic. Sauté for about 5 minutes until the vegetables begin to soften.
2. Stir in the rinsed lentils, ground cumin, ground coriander, smoked paprika, salt, and pepper. Cook for another 2 minutes to toast the spices.
3. Pour in the remaining vegetable broth and bring the soup to a boil.
4. Reduce the heat to low, cover, and simmer for about 20-25 minutes, or until the lentils are tender.
5. Stir in the fresh spinach leaves and lemon juice. Cook for an additional 2-3 minutes until the spinach wilts.
6. Taste and adjust the seasoning if needed.
7. Ladle the Lentil and Spinach Soup into bowls, garnish with fresh parsley if desired, and serve hot.
8. Enjoy your hearty soup!

Nutritional Information (per serving):
- Calories: 220
- Carbohydrates: 38g
- Protein: 13g
- Fat: 1g
- Fiber: 13g

- Sugar: 4g

Quinoa and Black Bean Salad

Intro: This Quinoa and Black Bean Salad is a nutrient-packed dish that's high in fiber and protein. It's a great choice for managing insulin resistance.
Total Time: 25 minutes

Ingredients:
- 1 cup quinoa, rinsed and drained
- 2 cups water or vegetable broth
- 1 can (15 ounces) black beans, drained and rinsed
- 1 cup corn kernels (fresh or frozen)
- 1 red bell pepper, diced
- 1/2 cup diced red onion
- 1/4 cup chopped fresh cilantro
- Juice of 2 limes
- 2 tablespoons olive oil
- 1 teaspoon ground cumin
- Salt and pepper to taste
- Avocado slices for garnish (optional)

Directions:
1. In a medium saucepan, combine the quinoa and water (or vegetable broth). Bring to a boil, then reduce the heat to low, cover, and simmer for 15-20 minutes, or until the quinoa is cooked and the liquid is absorbed. Remove from heat and fluff with a fork.
2. In a large mixing bowl, combine the cooked quinoa, black beans, corn kernels, diced red bell pepper, diced red onion, and chopped fresh cilantro.
3. In a separate small bowl, whisk together the lime juice, olive oil, ground cumin, salt, and pepper.
4. Pour the dressing over the quinoa and black bean mixture. Toss to combine and coat all the ingredients.
5. Taste and adjust the seasoning if needed.
6. Serve the Quinoa and Black Bean Salad in individual bowls, garnished with avocado slices if desired.
7. Enjoy your nutritious salad!

Nutritional Information (per serving):
- Calories: 320
- Carbohydrates: 53g
- Protein: 12g
- Fat: 8g
- Fiber: 11g
- Sugar: 3g

Tuna Salad Lettuce Wraps

Intro: These Tuna Salad Lettuce Wraps are a low-carb and protein-rich meal option that's perfect for managing insulin resistance.
Total Time: 15 minutes

Ingredients:
- 2 cans (5 ounces each) tuna in water, drained
- 1/4 cup diced celery
- 2 tablespoons diced red onion
- 2 tablespoons chopped dill pickles
- 1/4 cup plain Greek yogurt
- 1 tablespoon Dijon mustard
- 1 teaspoon lemon juice
- Salt and pepper to taste
- Butter lettuce leaves (or other large lettuce leaves) for wrapping
- Sliced tomatoes and cucumber for garnish (optional)

Directions:
1. In a mixing bowl, combine the drained tuna, diced celery, diced red onion, and chopped dill pickles.
2. In a separate small bowl, whisk together the plain Greek yogurt, Dijon mustard, lemon juice, salt, and pepper.
3. Pour the yogurt dressing over the tuna mixture and stir to combine.
4. Taste and adjust the seasoning if needed.
5. To assemble the wraps, place a spoonful of tuna salad onto a butter lettuce leaf.
6. Add sliced tomatoes and cucumber if desired.
7. Fold the sides of the lettuce leaf over the filling, then roll it up.

8. Repeat with the remaining lettuce leaves and tuna salad.
9. Serve your Tuna Salad Lettuce Wraps and enjoy!

Nutritional Information (per wrap):
- Calories: 100
- Carbohydrates: 3g
- Protein: 16g
- Fat: 2g
- Fiber: 1g
- Sugar: 1g

Greek Chicken Pita Pocket

Intro: Savor the flavors of Greece with this Greek Chicken Pita Pocket. It's a balanced meal with lean protein and fresh veggies that's suitable for managing insulin resistance.

Total Time: 30 minutes

Ingredients:
- 2 boneless, skinless chicken breasts
- 1 tablespoon olive oil
- 1 teaspoon dried oregano
- Salt and pepper to taste
- 4 whole wheat pita pockets
- 1 cup diced cucumber
- 1 cup diced tomatoes
- 1/2 cup diced red onion
- 1/4 cup crumbled feta cheese
- 1/4 cup plain Greek yogurt
- 1 tablespoon fresh lemon juice
- Fresh mint leaves for garnish (optional)

Directions:
1. Preheat your grill or grill pan to medium-high heat.
2. Brush the chicken breasts with olive oil and season with dried oregano, salt, and pepper.

3. Grill the chicken for about 6-7 minutes per side, or until it's cooked through and has grill marks. The internal temperature should reach 165°F (74°C).
4. Remove the chicken from the grill, let it rest for a few minutes, then slice it into thin strips.
5. In a bowl, combine the diced cucumber, diced tomatoes, diced red onion, and crumbled feta cheese.
6. In a separate small bowl, whisk together the plain Greek yogurt and fresh lemon juice.
7. Warm the whole wheat pita pockets in a dry skillet or microwave for about 10 seconds.
8. To assemble each pita pocket, spread a spoonful of the Greek yogurt dressing inside.
9. Add slices of grilled chicken and the cucumber-tomato-feta mixture.
10. Garnish with fresh mint leaves if desired.
11. Fold the pita pocket over the filling.
12. Serve your Greek Chicken Pita Pocket and enjoy!

Nutritional Information (per pita pocket):
- Calories: 320
- Carbohydrates: 32g
- Protein: 26g
- Fat: 10g
- Fiber: 5g
- Sugar: 5g

Broccoli and Cheddar Stuffed Sweet Potato

Intro: This Broccoli and Cheddar Stuffed Sweet Potato is a satisfying and fiber-rich meal that's suitable for managing insulin resistance.
Total Time: 50 minutes

Ingredients:
- 2 medium sweet potatoes
- 2 cups broccoli florets
- 1/2 cup shredded cheddar cheese
- Salt and pepper to taste
- Olive oil for drizzling

Directions:

1. Preheat your oven to 400°F (200°C).
2. Pierce the sweet potatoes with a fork a few times to allow steam to escape during baking.
3. Place the sweet potatoes on a baking sheet and bake for about 40-45 minutes, or until they are tender and can be easily pierced with a fork.
4. In the meantime, steam or boil the broccoli florets until they are tender, about 3-4 minutes. Drain and set aside.
5. Once the sweet potatoes are done, remove them from the oven and let them cool slightly.
6. Cut a slit lengthwise in each sweet potato, and carefully fluff the insides with a fork.
7. Season the sweet potato with salt and pepper to taste.
8. Fill each sweet potato with steamed broccoli florets and shredded cheddar cheese.
9. Return the stuffed sweet potatoes to the oven and bake for an additional 5-7 minutes, or until the cheese is melted and bubbly.
10. Drizzle with a bit of olive oil before serving.
11. Enjoy your Broccoli and Cheddar Stuffed Sweet Potato!

Nutritional Information (per stuffed sweet potato):

- Calories: 300
- Carbohydrates: 50g
- Protein: 11g
- Fat: 8g
- Fiber: 10g
- Sugar: 14g

Spinach and Strawberry Salad with Balsamic Vinaigrette

Intro: Indulge in the delightful combination of sweet and savory with this Spinach and Strawberry Salad. It's a low-sugar and high-fiber choice for managing insulin resistance.
Total Time: 15 minutes

Ingredients:

- 4 cups fresh spinach leaves

- 1 cup sliced strawberries
- 1/4 cup sliced almonds
- 1/4 cup crumbled goat cheese
- 2 tablespoons balsamic vinaigrette dressing

Directions:
1. In a large salad bowl, arrange the fresh spinach leaves.
2. Top the spinach with sliced strawberries, sliced almonds, and crumbled goat cheese.
3. Drizzle the salad with balsamic vinaigrette dressing.
4. Toss the salad gently to combine all the ingredients.
5. Serve your Spinach and Strawberry Salad and enjoy!

Nutritional Information (per serving):
- Calories: 180
- Carbohydrates: 10g
- Protein: 6g
- Fat: 14g
- Fiber: 3g
- Sugar: 5g

Cauliflower and Chickpea Curry

Intro: This Cauliflower and Chickpea Curry is a flavorful and satisfying dish that's rich in fiber and plant-based protein. It's a great choice for managing insulin resistance.
Total Time: 30 minutes

Ingredients:
- 1 cauliflower head, cut into florets
- 1 can (15 ounces) chickpeas, drained and rinsed
- 1 onion, chopped
- 3 cloves garlic, minced
- 1 tablespoon olive oil
- 1 can (14 ounces) diced tomatoes
- 1 can (14 ounces) coconut milk
- 2 tablespoons curry powder

- 1 teaspoon ground turmeric
- 1/2 teaspoon ground cumin
- Salt and pepper to taste
- Fresh cilantro leaves for garnish (optional)
- Cooked brown rice or quinoa for serving (optional)

Directions:

1. In a large skillet or pot, heat olive oil over medium heat. Add chopped onion and sauté until it becomes translucent, about 2-3 minutes.
2. Add minced garlic, curry powder, ground turmeric, and ground cumin to the skillet. Cook for another 2 minutes to toast the spices.
3. Stir in the cauliflower florets and chickpeas, coating them with the spice mixture.
4. Pour in the diced tomatoes (with their juice) and coconut milk. Season with salt and pepper.
5. Bring the mixture to a boil, then reduce the heat to low, cover, and simmer for about 15-20 minutes, or until the cauliflower is tender.
6. Taste and adjust the seasoning if needed.
7. Serve your Cauliflower and Chickpea Curry as-is or over cooked brown rice or quinoa.
8. Garnish with fresh cilantro leaves if desired.
9. Enjoy your flavorful curry!

Nutritional Information (per serving, without rice or quinoa):

- Calories: 300
- Carbohydrates: 22g
- Protein: 9g
- Fat: 20g
- Fiber: 8g
- Sugar: 6g

Turkey and Quinoa Stuffed Bell Peppers

Intro: These Turkey and Quinoa Stuffed Bell Peppers are a balanced and fiber-rich meal option that's suitable for managing insulin resistance.
Total Time: 45 minutes

Ingredients:

- 4 large bell peppers (any color)
- 1 cup quinoa, rinsed and drained
- 2 cups water or vegetable broth
- 1 pound lean ground turkey
- 1/2 cup diced onions
- 1/2 cup diced tomatoes
- 1/2 cup tomato sauce
- 1 teaspoon dried Italian seasoning
- Salt and pepper to taste
- 1/4 cup shredded mozzarella cheese (optional)
- Fresh basil leaves for garnish (optional)

Directions:

1. Preheat your oven to 375°F (190°C).
2. Cut the tops off the bell peppers and remove the seeds and membranes. Set aside.
3. In a medium saucepan, combine the quinoa and water (or vegetable broth). Bring to a boil, then reduce the heat to low, cover, and simmer for 15-20 minutes, or until the quinoa is cooked and the liquid is absorbed. Remove from heat and fluff with a fork.
4. In a large skillet, cook the lean ground turkey over medium-high heat until it's no longer pink, breaking it into small pieces as it cooks.
5. Add diced onions to the skillet and sauté for about 3-4 minutes until they become translucent.
6. Stir in diced tomatoes, tomato sauce, dried Italian seasoning, salt, and pepper. Cook for another 2 minutes to combine the flavors.
7. Add the cooked quinoa to the turkey mixture and stir until everything is well combined.
8. Stuff each bell pepper with the turkey and quinoa mixture.
9. Place the stuffed bell peppers in a baking dish. If desired, sprinkle shredded mozzarella cheese on top of each stuffed pepper.
10. Cover the baking dish with aluminum foil and bake for about 20-25 minutes, or until the peppers are tender.
11. Garnish with fresh basil leaves if desired.
12. Serve your Turkey and Quinoa Stuffed Bell Peppers.
13. Enjoy your wholesome meal!

Nutritional Information (per stuffed bell pepper, without cheese):
- Calories: 330
- Carbohydrates: 38g
- Protein: 26g
- Fat: 9g
- Fiber: 6g
- Sugar: 7g

Caprese Salad with Fresh Mozzarella

Intro: Indulge in the classic flavors of Italy with this Caprese Salad featuring fresh mozzarella, ripe tomatoes, and fragrant basil. It's a light and refreshing option for managing insulin resistance.
Total Time: 10 minutes

Ingredients:
- 2 large tomatoes, sliced
- 8 ounces fresh mozzarella cheese, sliced
- Fresh basil leaves
- 2 tablespoons extra-virgin olive oil
- 2 tablespoons balsamic glaze
- Salt and pepper to taste

Directions:
1. Arrange the tomato and mozzarella slices on a serving platter, alternating them.
2. Tuck fresh basil leaves between the tomato and mozzarella slices.
3. Drizzle extra-virgin olive oil and balsamic glaze over the salad.
4. Season with salt and pepper to taste.
5. Serve your Caprese Salad with Fresh Mozzarella immediately and enjoy!

Nutritional Information (per serving):
- Calories: 300
- Carbohydrates: 7g
- Protein: 14g
- Fat: 24g
- Fiber: 2g

* Sugar: 4g

Lemon Herb Grilled Shrimp Skewers

Intro: These Lemon Herb Grilled Shrimp Skewers are a flavorful and protein-packed option that's perfect for managing insulin resistance.
Total Time: 20 minutes

Ingredients:
* 1 pound large shrimp, peeled and deveined
* 2 cloves garlic, minced
* Zest and juice of 1 lemon
* 2 tablespoons fresh parsley, chopped
* 1 tablespoon fresh basil, chopped
* 1 tablespoon olive oil
* Salt and pepper to taste
* Wooden skewers, soaked in water for 30 minutes

Directions:
1. In a bowl, combine minced garlic, lemon zest, lemon juice, fresh parsley, fresh basil, olive oil, salt, and pepper. Mix well to create the marinade.
2. Thread the peeled and deveined shrimp onto the wooden skewers.
3. Brush the shrimp skewers with the marinade, ensuring they are well coated.
4. Preheat your grill or grill pan to medium-high heat.
5. Grill the shrimp skewers for about 2-3 minutes per side, or until they are opaque and grill marks appear.
6. Remove the shrimp skewers from the grill and serve hot.
7. Enjoy your Lemon Herb Grilled Shrimp Skewers!

Nutritional Information (per serving):
* Calories: 150
* Carbohydrates: 2g
* Protein: 24g
* Fat: 6g
* Fiber: 0g
* Sugar: 0g

Asian-Inspired Tofu Stir-Fry

Intro: This Asian-Inspired Tofu Stir-Fry is loaded with vegetables and tofu in a savory sauce. It's a balanced meal choice for managing insulin resistance.
Total Time: 25 minutes

Ingredients:
- 14 ounces extra-firm tofu, cubed
- 2 tablespoons low-sodium soy sauce
- 1 tablespoon sesame oil
- 1 tablespoon rice vinegar
- 1 tablespoon honey or maple syrup
- 1 teaspoon fresh ginger, minced
- 2 cloves garlic, minced
- 1 tablespoon vegetable oil
- 1 bell pepper, thinly sliced
- 1 cup broccoli florets
- 1 cup snap peas
- 1 carrot, thinly sliced
- 2 cups cooked brown rice
- Sesame seeds for garnish (optional)
- Green onions, chopped, for garnish (optional)

Directions:
1. In a bowl, combine cubed tofu, low-sodium soy sauce, sesame oil, rice vinegar, honey or maple syrup, minced ginger, and minced garlic. Allow the tofu to marinate for about 10 minutes.
2. In a wok or large skillet, heat vegetable oil over medium-high heat.
3. Add marinated tofu to the skillet and cook for about 2-3 minutes per side, or until the tofu is lightly browned and slightly crispy. Remove tofu from the skillet and set it aside.
4. In the same skillet, add bell pepper, broccoli florets, snap peas, and thinly sliced carrot. Stir-fry for about 4-5 minutes until the vegetables are tender-crisp.
5. Return the cooked tofu to the skillet and toss everything together to heat through.
6. Serve the stir-fry over cooked brown rice.

7. Garnish with sesame seeds and chopped green onions if desired.
8. Enjoy your Asian-Inspired Tofu Stir-Fry!

Nutritional Information (per serving, excluding garnishes):
- Calories: 320
- Carbohydrates: 45g
- Protein: 15g
- Fat: 10g
- Fiber: 6g
- Sugar: 8g

Zoodle (Zucchini Noodle) Primavera

Intro: Indulge in a low-carb twist on a classic Italian dish with this Zoodle (Zucchini Noodle) Primavera. It's rich in vegetables and flavor, making it a great choice for managing insulin resistance.
Total Time: 20 minutes

Ingredients:
- 4 medium zucchinis, spiralized into noodles (zoodles)
- 2 tablespoons olive oil
- 2 cloves garlic, minced
- 1 cup cherry tomatoes, halved
- 1 cup bell peppers, thinly sliced (any color)
- 1 cup broccoli florets
- 1/2 cup grated Parmesan cheese
- 1/4 cup fresh basil leaves, chopped
- Salt and pepper to taste
- Red pepper flakes for added heat (optional)

Directions:
1. Heat olive oil in a large skillet over medium heat. Add minced garlic and sauté for about 30 seconds until fragrant.
2. Add cherry tomatoes, bell peppers, and broccoli florets to the skillet. Sauté for about 5 minutes, or until the vegetables are tender-crisp.

3. Add zucchini noodles (zoodles) to the skillet and toss to combine with the cooked vegetables. Sauté for an additional 2-3 minutes until the zoodles are heated through.
4. Remove the skillet from heat and stir in grated Parmesan cheese and chopped fresh basil.
5. Season with salt and pepper to taste. If you like a bit of heat, add red pepper flakes.
6. Serve your Zoodle Primavera immediately.
7. Enjoy this low-carb twist on a classic!

Nutritional Information (per serving):
- Calories: 180
- Carbohydrates: 10g
- Protein: 9g
- Fat: 13g
- Fiber: 3g
- Sugar: 6g

Chickpea and Vegetable Quinoa Bowl

Intro: This Chickpea and Vegetable Quinoa Bowl is a nutrient-packed meal that's high in fiber and plant-based protein. It's an excellent choice for managing insulin resistance.
Total Time: 30 minutes

Ingredients:
- 1 cup quinoa, rinsed and drained
- 2 cups water or vegetable broth
- 1 can (15 ounces) chickpeas, drained and rinsed
- 2 cups broccoli florets
- 1 red bell pepper, diced
- 1 yellow bell pepper, diced
- 1/2 cup cherry tomatoes, halved
- 1/4 cup diced red onion
- 1/4 cup chopped fresh parsley
- 2 tablespoons olive oil
- Juice of 1 lemon

- 1 teaspoon ground cumin
- Salt and pepper to taste
- Crumbled feta cheese for garnish (optional)

Directions:
1. In a medium saucepan, combine the quinoa and water (or vegetable broth). Bring to a boil, then reduce the heat to low, cover, and simmer for 15-20 minutes, or until the quinoa is cooked and the liquid is absorbed. Remove from heat and fluff with a fork.
2. In a large mixing bowl, combine the cooked quinoa, chickpeas, broccoli florets, diced red and yellow bell peppers, halved cherry tomatoes, and diced red onion.
3. In a separate small bowl, whisk together olive oil, lemon juice, ground cumin, salt, and pepper.
4. Pour the dressing over the quinoa and vegetable mixture. Toss to combine and coat all the ingredients.
5. Stir in chopped fresh parsley.
6. Serve the Chickpea and Vegetable Quinoa Bowl in individual bowls.
7. Garnish with crumbled feta cheese if desired.
8. Enjoy this nutritious and colorful bowl!

Nutritional Information (per serving, excluding feta cheese):
- Calories: 320
- Carbohydrates: 55g
- Protein: 12g
- Fat: 7g
- Fiber: 9g
- Sugar: 6g

Roasted Red Pepper and Hummus Wrap

Intro: This Roasted Red Pepper and Hummus Wrap is a delightful combination of flavors and textures. It's a satisfying choice for managing insulin resistance.
Total Time: 15 minutes

Ingredients:
- 4 whole wheat tortillas or wraps
- 1 cup roasted red peppers (from a jar), drained and sliced

- 1 cup baby spinach leaves
- 1/2 cup store-bought hummus
- 1/4 cup crumbled feta cheese
- Kalamata olives, pitted and sliced, for added flavor (optional)

Directions:
1. Lay out the whole wheat tortillas or wraps on a clean surface.
2. Spread a generous layer of hummus onto each tortilla, leaving a border around the edges.
3. Divide the roasted red pepper slices, baby spinach leaves, and crumbled feta cheese evenly among the tortillas.
4. If desired, add sliced Kalamata olives for extra flavor.
5. Carefully fold in the sides of each tortilla, then roll it up tightly from the bottom, creating a wrap.
6. Slice each wrap in half diagonally if preferred.
7. Serve your Roasted Red Pepper and Hummus Wrap.
8. Enjoy this tasty and nutritious wrap!

Nutritional Information (per wrap):
- Calories: 250
- Carbohydrates: 34g
- Protein: 8g
- Fat: 9g
- Fiber: 7g
- Sugar: 3g

Salmon and Quinoa Salad with Dill Dressing

Intro: This Salmon and Quinoa Salad with Dill Dressing is a protein-packed and omega-3-rich meal option that's suitable for managing insulin resistance.
Total Time: 25 minutes

Ingredients:
- 2 salmon fillets
- 1 cup quinoa, rinsed and drained
- 2 cups water or vegetable broth
- 1 cup cucumber, diced

- 1 cup cherry tomatoes, halved
- 1/4 cup red onion, finely chopped
- 1/4 cup fresh dill, chopped
- Juice of 1 lemon
- 2 tablespoons olive oil
- Salt and pepper to taste
- Lemon wedges for garnish (optional)

Directions:

1. Preheat your oven to 400°F (200°C).
2. Place the salmon fillets on a baking sheet lined with parchment paper. Season with salt and pepper.
3. Bake the salmon in the preheated oven for about 15-20 minutes, or until it flakes easily with a fork.
4. In a medium saucepan, combine the quinoa and water (or vegetable broth). Bring to a boil, then reduce the heat to low, cover, and simmer for 15-20 minutes, or until the quinoa is cooked and the liquid is absorbed. Remove from heat and fluff with a fork.
5. In a large mixing bowl, combine the cooked quinoa, diced cucumber, halved cherry tomatoes, finely chopped red onion, and chopped fresh dill.
6. In a separate small bowl, whisk together lemon juice and olive oil. Season with salt and pepper to taste.
7. Pour the lemon dill dressing over the quinoa and vegetable mixture. Toss to combine and coat all the ingredients.
8. Divide the quinoa salad onto plates.
9. Top each salad with a baked salmon fillet.
10. Garnish with lemon wedges if desired.
11. Enjoy your Salmon and Quinoa Salad with Dill Dressing!

Nutritional Information (per serving):

- Calories: 380
- Carbohydrates: 32g
- Protein: 30g
- Fat: 15g
- Fiber: 4g
- Sugar: 3g

Ratatouille with Brown Rice

Intro: This Ratatouille with Brown Rice is a flavorful and vegetable-packed dish that's perfect for managing insulin resistance.

Total Time: 45 minutes

Ingredients:
- 1 cup brown rice, rinsed and drained
- 2 cups water or vegetable broth
- 2 tablespoons olive oil
- 1 onion, diced
- 2 cloves garlic, minced
- 1 eggplant, diced
- 2 zucchinis, diced
- 1 red bell pepper, diced
- 1 yellow bell pepper, diced
- 1 can (14 ounces) diced tomatoes
- 1 teaspoon dried thyme
- 1 teaspoon dried rosemary
- Salt and pepper to taste
- Fresh basil leaves for garnish (optional)

Directions:
1. In a medium saucepan, combine the brown rice and water (or vegetable broth). Bring to a boil, then reduce the heat to low, cover, and simmer for 35-40 minutes, or until the rice is cooked and the liquid is absorbed. Remove from heat and fluff with a fork.
2. In a large skillet, heat olive oil over medium heat. Add diced onion and minced garlic. Sauté for about 2-3 minutes until the onion becomes translucent.
3. Add diced eggplant, diced zucchinis, diced red bell pepper, and diced yellow bell pepper to the skillet. Cook for about 5-7 minutes, or until the vegetables start to soften.
4. Stir in diced tomatoes (with their juice), dried thyme, dried rosemary, salt, and pepper. Cook for an additional 5 minutes to combine the flavors.
5. Serve the Ratatouille over cooked brown rice.
6. Garnish with fresh basil leaves if desired.

7. Enjoy this flavorful and hearty dish!

Nutritional Information (per serving, excluding garnish):
- Calories: 300
- Carbohydrates: 58g
- Protein: 6g
- Fat: 7g
- Fiber: 9g
- Sugar: 7g

Kale and Quinoa Stuffed Portobello Mushrooms

Intro: These Kale and Quinoa Stuffed Portobello Mushrooms are a nutritious and savory dish that's perfect for managing insulin resistance.
Total Time: 30 minutes

Ingredients:
- 4 large Portobello mushrooms
- 1 cup quinoa, rinsed and drained
- 2 cups water or vegetable broth
- 2 tablespoons olive oil
- 1 onion, chopped
- 2 cloves garlic, minced
- 4 cups kale leaves, stems removed and chopped
- 1/4 cup grated Parmesan cheese
- Salt and pepper to taste

Directions:
1. Preheat your oven to 375°F (190°C).
2. Remove the stems from the Portobello mushrooms and gently scrape out the gills using a spoon. Set aside.
3. In a medium saucepan, combine the quinoa and water (or vegetable broth). Bring to a boil, then reduce the heat to low, cover, and simmer for 15-20 minutes, or until the quinoa is cooked and the liquid is absorbed. Remove from heat and fluff with a fork.

4. In a large skillet, heat olive oil over medium heat. Add chopped onion and minced garlic. Sauté for about 2-3 minutes until the onion becomes translucent.
5. Add chopped kale to the skillet and cook for about 3-4 minutes until it wilts and becomes tender.
6. Stir in cooked quinoa and grated Parmesan cheese. Season with salt and pepper to taste. Mix everything well.
7. Place the Portobello mushrooms on a baking sheet lined with parchment paper.
8. Fill each mushroom cap with the kale and quinoa mixture, pressing it down gently.
9. Bake the stuffed Portobello mushrooms in the preheated oven for about 15 minutes, or until the mushrooms are tender and the stuffing is heated through.
10. Serve your Kale and Quinoa Stuffed Portobello Mushrooms.
11. Enjoy this nutritious and flavorful dish!

Nutritional Information (per stuffed mushroom):
- Calories: 200
- Carbohydrates: 29g
- Protein: 9g
- Fat: 6g
- Fiber: 4g
- Sugar: 3g

Thai Coconut Soup with Shrimp

Intro: Indulge in the rich and aromatic flavors of Thailand with this Thai Coconut Soup with Shrimp. It's a comforting and satisfying option for managing insulin resistance.
Total Time: 30 minutes

Ingredients:
- 1 tablespoon vegetable oil
- 1 onion, chopped
- 2 cloves garlic, minced
- 2 tablespoons Thai red curry paste
- 1 can (14 ounces) coconut milk

- 4 cups low-sodium chicken broth or vegetable broth
- 1 pound large shrimp, peeled and deveined
- 1 cup sliced mushrooms
- 1 red bell pepper, thinly sliced
- 1 carrot, thinly sliced
- Juice of 2 limes
- 2 tablespoons fish sauce (optional)
- Fresh cilantro leaves for garnish (optional)
- Red chili flakes for added heat (optional)

Directions:
1. In a large pot, heat vegetable oil over medium heat. Add chopped onion and sauté for about 2-3 minutes until the onion becomes translucent.
2. Add minced garlic and Thai red curry paste to the pot. Cook for another 2 minutes to toast the spices.
3. Pour in coconut milk and chicken broth (or vegetable broth). Stir to combine and bring the mixture to a simmer.
4. Add peeled and deveined shrimp, sliced mushrooms, thinly sliced red bell pepper, and thinly sliced carrot to the pot. Simmer for about 5-7 minutes, or until the shrimp turn pink and the vegetables are tender.
5. Stir in lime juice and fish sauce (if using). Taste and adjust the seasoning if needed. If you prefer some heat, add red chili flakes.
6. Serve your Thai Coconut Soup with Shrimp.
7. Garnish with fresh cilantro leaves if desired.
8. Enjoy this aromatic and comforting soup!

Nutritional Information (per serving, excluding garnishes):
- Calories: 280
- Carbohydrates: 12g
- Protein: 21g
- Fat: 18g
- Fiber: 2g
- Sugar: 3g

Pesto Pasta with Whole Wheat Spaghetti

Intro: This Pesto Pasta with Whole Wheat Spaghetti is a simple yet satisfying dish that's suitable for managing insulin resistance. The whole wheat pasta provides added fiber.

Total Time: 20 minutes

Ingredients:
- 8 ounces whole wheat spaghetti
- 1/2 cup store-bought or homemade basil pesto
- 1 cup cherry tomatoes, halved
- 1/4 cup grated Parmesan cheese
- Fresh basil leaves for garnish (optional)
- Pine nuts for garnish (optional)

Directions:
1. Cook the whole wheat spaghetti according to the package instructions until al dente. Drain and set aside.
2. In a large mixing bowl, combine the cooked spaghetti and basil pesto. Toss to coat the pasta evenly.
3. Add halved cherry tomatoes and grated Parmesan cheese to the pasta. Toss again to combine.
4. Serve your Pesto Pasta with Whole Wheat Spaghetti.
5. Garnish with fresh basil leaves and pine nuts if desired.
6. Enjoy this simple and flavorful pasta dish!

Nutritional Information (per serving, excluding garnishes):
- Calories: 350
- Carbohydrates: 42g
- Protein: 10g
- Fat: 17g
- Fiber: 7g
- Sugar: 2g

Baked Salmon with Asparagus

Intro: This Baked Salmon with Asparagus is a simple and nutritious dish that's rich in omega-3 fatty acids and perfect for managing insulin resistance.

Total Time: 25 minutes

Ingredients:
- 4 salmon fillets
- 1 bunch asparagus, trimmed
- 2 tablespoons olive oil
- 2 cloves garlic, minced
- Zest and juice of 1 lemon
- Salt and pepper to taste
- Fresh dill for garnish (optional)

Directions:
1. Preheat your oven to 375°F (190°C).
2. Place the salmon fillets and trimmed asparagus on a baking sheet lined with parchment paper.
3. In a small bowl, whisk together olive oil, minced garlic, lemon zest, lemon juice, salt, and pepper.
4. Drizzle the lemon garlic mixture evenly over the salmon and asparagus.
5. Bake in the preheated oven for about 15-18 minutes, or until the salmon is cooked through and flakes easily with a fork.
6. Garnish with fresh dill if desired.
7. Serve your Baked Salmon with Asparagus hot.
8. Enjoy this flavorful and healthy dish!

Nutritional Information (per serving):
- Calories: 300
- Carbohydrates: 4g
- Protein: 30g
- Fat: 20g
- Fiber: 2g
- Sugar: 1g

Spaghetti Squash and Turkey Meatballs

Intro: This Spaghetti Squash and Turkey Meatballs dish is a low-carb alternative to traditional spaghetti and meatballs, making it a suitable choice for managing insulin resistance.

Total Time: 50 minutes

Ingredients: *For the Spaghetti Squash:*
- 2 spaghetti squash
- 2 tablespoons olive oil
- Salt and pepper to taste

For the Turkey Meatballs:
- 1 pound ground turkey
- 1/4 cup whole wheat breadcrumbs
- 1/4 cup grated Parmesan cheese
- 1/4 cup chopped fresh parsley
- 1 egg
- 2 cloves garlic, minced
- 1 teaspoon Italian seasoning
- Salt and pepper to taste

For the Tomato Sauce:
- 1 can (14 ounces) crushed tomatoes
- 2 cloves garlic, minced
- 1 teaspoon dried basil
- Salt and pepper to taste

Directions: *For the Spaghetti Squash:*
1. Preheat your oven to 400°F (200°C).
2. Slice the spaghetti squash in half lengthwise and scoop out the seeds.
3. Drizzle each half with olive oil and season with salt and pepper.
4. Place the squash halves cut-side down on a baking sheet lined with parchment paper.
5. Roast in the preheated oven for about 35-40 minutes, or until the squash flesh can be easily scraped into "spaghetti" with a fork.
6. Once done, use a fork to scrape the squash into strands.

For the Turkey Meatballs:
1. In a mixing bowl, combine ground turkey, whole wheat breadcrumbs, grated Parmesan cheese, chopped fresh parsley, egg, minced garlic, Italian seasoning, salt, and pepper. Mix well.
2. Shape the mixture into meatballs, about 1 to 1.5 inches in diameter.
3. Heat a skillet over medium-high heat and add a bit of olive oil.
4. Cook the turkey meatballs in the skillet, turning them to brown evenly on all sides. This should take about 8-10 minutes. Once cooked through, remove from heat and set aside.

For the Tomato Sauce:
1. In a saucepan, combine crushed tomatoes, minced garlic, dried basil, salt, and pepper. Simmer for about 5-7 minutes to heat through and combine the flavors.

To Assemble:
1. Serve the spaghetti squash strands topped with tomato sauce and turkey meatballs.
2. Garnish with additional grated Parmesan cheese and fresh parsley if desired.
3. Enjoy your Spaghetti Squash and Turkey Meatballs!

Nutritional Information (per serving, excluding garnishes):
- Calories: 320
- Carbohydrates: 18g
- Protein: 30g
- Fat: 15g
- Fiber: 4g
- Sugar: 6g

Lemon Garlic Roasted Chicken

Intro: This Lemon Garlic Roasted Chicken is a savory and tangy dish that's packed with flavor. It's a great option for managing insulin resistance.
Total Time: 1 hour

Ingredients:
- 4 bone-in, skin-on chicken thighs
- 2 tablespoons olive oil
- Zest and juice of 1 lemon
- 4 cloves garlic, minced
- 1 teaspoon dried oregano
- Salt and pepper to taste
- Fresh parsley for garnish (optional)

Directions:
1. Preheat your oven to 375°F (190°C).
2. In a small bowl, whisk together olive oil, lemon zest, lemon juice, minced garlic, dried oregano, salt, and pepper.
3. Place the chicken thighs in a baking dish.
4. Pour the lemon garlic mixture over the chicken thighs, ensuring they are well coated.
5. Roast in the preheated oven for about 45-50 minutes, or until the chicken is cooked through and the skin is crispy.
6. Garnish with fresh parsley if desired.
7. Serve your Lemon Garlic Roasted Chicken hot.
8. Enjoy this flavorful and aromatic dish!

Nutritional Information (per serving):
- Calories: 350
- Carbohydrates: 2g
- Protein: 28g
- Fat: 25g
- Fiber: 0g
- Sugar: 0g

Beef and Broccoli Stir-Fry

Intro: This Beef and Broccoli Stir-Fry is a quick and flavorful dish that's rich in protein and low in carbohydrates, making it suitable for managing insulin resistance.

Total Time: 30 minutes

Ingredients:

- 1 pound flank steak, thinly sliced
- 1/4 cup low-sodium soy sauce
- 2 tablespoons hoisin sauce
- 1 tablespoon rice vinegar
- 1 tablespoon honey or maple syrup
- 2 cloves garlic, minced
- 1 teaspoon fresh ginger, minced
- 2 tablespoons vegetable oil
- 4 cups broccoli florets
- 1 red bell pepper, thinly sliced
- 2 green onions, chopped
- Sesame seeds for garnish (optional)

Directions:

1. In a bowl, combine thinly sliced flank steak, low-sodium soy sauce, hoisin sauce, rice vinegar, honey or maple syrup, minced garlic, and minced ginger. Allow the beef to marinate for about 10 minutes.
2. Heat vegetable oil in a large skillet or wok over high heat.
3. Add marinated beef to the skillet and stir-fry for about 3-4 minutes until it's browned and cooked to your desired level of doneness. Remove beef from the skillet and set aside.
4. In the same skillet, add broccoli florets and thinly sliced red bell pepper. Stir-fry for about 3-4 minutes until the vegetables are tender-crisp.
5. Return the cooked beef to the skillet and toss everything together to heat through.
6. Garnish with chopped green onions and sesame seeds if desired.
7. Serve your Beef and Broccoli Stir-Fry hot.
8. Enjoy this savory and satisfying stir-fry!

Nutritional Information (per serving, excluding garnishes):

- Calories: 320
- Carbohydrates: 15g
- Protein: 28g
- Fat: 16g
- Fiber: 4g
- Sugar: 8g

Cauliflower and Lentil Curry

Intro: This Cauliflower and Lentil Curry is a flavorful and hearty plant-based dish that's perfect for managing insulin resistance.

Total Time: 40 minutes

Ingredients:
- 1 head cauliflower, cut into florets
- 1 cup dried green or brown lentils, rinsed and drained
- 1 onion, chopped
- 2 cloves garlic, minced
- 1 tablespoon olive oil
- 2 tablespoons curry powder
- 1 can (14 ounces) diced tomatoes
- 1 can (14 ounces) coconut milk
- Salt and pepper to taste
- Fresh cilantro leaves for garnish (optional)

Directions:
1. Heat olive oil in a large pot over medium heat. Add chopped onion and sauté for about 2-3 minutes until the onion becomes translucent.
2. Add minced garlic and curry powder to the pot. Cook for another 2 minutes to toast the spices.
3. Stir in cauliflower florets, dried lentils, diced tomatoes (with their juice), and coconut milk. Add salt and pepper to taste.
4. Bring the mixture to a simmer, then reduce the heat to low, cover, and cook for about 25-30 minutes, or until the lentils are tender and the cauliflower is cooked.
5. Taste and adjust the seasoning if needed.
6. Garnish with fresh cilantro leaves if desired.
7. Serve your Cauliflower and Lentil Curry hot.
8. Enjoy this flavorful and comforting curry!

Nutritional Information (per serving, excluding garnish):
- Calories: 350
- Carbohydrates: 42g
- Protein: 14g

- Fat: 17g
- Fiber: 16g
- Sugar: 9g

Stuffed Bell Peppers with Ground Turkey

Intro: These Stuffed Bell Peppers with Ground Turkey are a delicious and nutritious option for managing insulin resistance.
Total Time: 1 hour

Ingredients:
- 4 large bell peppers, any color
- 1 pound ground turkey
- 1 cup cooked brown rice
- 1 can (14 ounces) diced tomatoes
- 1/2 cup diced onion
- 1/2 cup diced celery
- 1/2 cup diced carrot
- 2 cloves garlic, minced
- 1 teaspoon dried oregano
- Salt and pepper to taste
- Grated mozzarella cheese for topping (optional)
- Fresh basil leaves for garnish (optional)

Directions:
1. Preheat your oven to 375°F (190°C).
2. Cut the tops off the bell peppers and remove the seeds and membranes. Set aside.
3. In a skillet, cook ground turkey over medium heat until browned and cooked through. Break it into smaller pieces as it cooks.
4. Add diced onion, diced celery, diced carrot, and minced garlic to the skillet with the turkey. Sauté for about 5 minutes, or until the vegetables are softened.
5. Stir in cooked brown rice, diced tomatoes (with their juice), dried oregano, salt, and pepper. Mix everything well.
6. Stuff each bell pepper with the turkey and rice mixture, packing it down firmly.

7. Place the stuffed bell peppers in a baking dish and cover with aluminum foil.
8. Bake in the preheated oven for about 25-30 minutes, or until the bell peppers are tender.
9. If desired, remove the foil, top each stuffed bell pepper with grated mozzarella cheese, and bake for an additional 5 minutes, or until the cheese is melted and bubbly.
10. Garnish with fresh basil leaves if desired.
11. Serve your Stuffed Bell Peppers with Ground Turkey hot.
12. Enjoy this comforting and satisfying dish!

Nutritional Information (per stuffed bell pepper, excluding garnishes):

- Calories: 350
- Carbohydrates: 29g
- Protein: 28g
- Fat: 12g
- Fiber: 6g
- Sugar: 8g

Grilled Eggplant Parmesan

Intro: This Grilled Eggplant Parmesan is a lighter and low-carb twist on the classic dish. It's a flavorful option for managing insulin resistance.
Total Time: 40 minutes

Ingredients:

- 2 large eggplants, sliced lengthwise into 1/2-inch thick slices
- 2 cups marinara sauce (store-bought or homemade)
- 1 cup part-skim mozzarella cheese, shredded
- 1/2 cup grated Parmesan cheese
- 1/4 cup fresh basil leaves, chopped
- 1/4 cup fresh parsley leaves, chopped
- 2 cloves garlic, minced
- Olive oil for brushing eggplant slices
- Salt and pepper to taste
- Red pepper flakes for added heat (optional)

Directions:

1. Preheat your grill to medium-high heat.
2. Brush eggplant slices lightly with olive oil and season with salt and pepper.
3. Grill the eggplant slices for about 2-3 minutes per side, or until they have grill marks and are tender. Remove from the grill and set aside.
4. In a mixing bowl, combine chopped fresh basil, chopped fresh parsley, minced garlic, and red pepper flakes (if using) with the marinara sauce.
5. Preheat your oven to 375°F (190°C).
6. In a baking dish, spread a thin layer of marinara sauce on the bottom.
7. Place a layer of grilled eggplant slices on top of the sauce.
8. Sprinkle shredded mozzarella cheese and grated Parmesan cheese over the eggplant slices.
9. Repeat the layers, finishing with a layer of cheese on top.
10. Cover the baking dish with aluminum foil.
11. Bake in the preheated oven for about 20-25 minutes, or until the cheese is melted and bubbly.
12. Remove the foil and bake for an additional 5 minutes, or until the cheese is golden brown.
13. Serve your Grilled Eggplant Parmesan hot.
14. Enjoy this lighter take on a classic Italian favorite!

Nutritional Information (per serving, excluding garnishes):

- Calories: 250
- Carbohydrates: 22g
- Protein: 12g
- Fat: 14g
- Fiber: 8g
- Sugar: 11g

Shrimp and Zucchini Noodle Scampi

Intro: This Shrimp and Zucchini Noodle Scampi is a low-carb and flavorful dish that's perfect for managing insulin resistance.
Total Time: 20 minutes

Ingredients:

- 1 pound large shrimp, peeled and deveined

- 4 medium zucchinis, spiralized into noodles
- 3 tablespoons unsalted butter
- 4 cloves garlic, minced
- Zest and juice of 1 lemon
- Red pepper flakes for added heat (optional)
- Salt and pepper to taste
- Fresh parsley leaves for garnish (optional)
- Grated Parmesan cheese for garnish (optional)

Directions:
1. In a large skillet, melt unsalted butter over medium-high heat.
2. Add minced garlic and red pepper flakes (if using) to the skillet. Sauté for about 1 minute until the garlic becomes fragrant.
3. Add peeled and deveined shrimp to the skillet. Cook for about 2-3 minutes per side, or until the shrimp turn pink and opaque. Remove from the skillet and set aside.
4. In the same skillet, add spiralized zucchini noodles. Sauté for about 2-3 minutes until they are tender-crisp.
5. Return the cooked shrimp to the skillet with the zucchini noodles.
6. Add lemon zest and lemon juice to the skillet. Season with salt and pepper to taste. Toss everything together to heat through.
7. Serve your Shrimp and Zucchini Noodle Scampi hot.
8. Garnish with fresh parsley leaves and grated Parmesan cheese if desired.
9. Enjoy this light and flavorful dish!

Nutritional Information (per serving, excluding garnishes):
- Calories: 250
- Carbohydrates: 8g
- Protein: 26g
- Fat: 13g
- Fiber: 2g
- Sugar: 4g

BBQ Pulled Chicken Sandwich

Intro: This BBQ Pulled Chicken Sandwich is a satisfying and flavorful meal that's suitable for managing insulin resistance.

Total Time: 30 minutes

Ingredients:
- 2 boneless, skinless chicken breasts
- 1 cup low-sugar barbecue sauce
- 1/2 cup low-sodium chicken broth
- 1 onion, thinly sliced
- 2 cloves garlic, minced
- Whole wheat hamburger buns or rolls
- Coleslaw (store-bought or homemade) for topping
- Pickles for garnish (optional)

Directions:
1. Place chicken breasts in a slow cooker.
2. In a mixing bowl, combine low-sugar barbecue sauce, low-sodium chicken broth, thinly sliced onion, and minced garlic. Mix well.
3. Pour the barbecue sauce mixture over the chicken breasts in the slow cooker.
4. Cover and cook on low for 6-8 hours or on high for 3-4 hours, or until the chicken is tender and can be easily shredded with a fork.
5. Remove the cooked chicken from the slow cooker and shred it with two forks.
6. Return the shredded chicken to the slow cooker and mix it with the barbecue sauce.
7. Serve your BBQ Pulled Chicken on whole wheat hamburger buns or rolls.
8. Top with coleslaw and garnish with pickles if desired.
9. Enjoy this delicious and saucy sandwich!

Nutritional Information (per sandwich, excluding garnishes):
- Calories: 300
- Carbohydrates: 30g
- Protein: 28g
- Fat: 7g
- Fiber: 4g
- Sugar: 10g

Tofu and Vegetable Kebabs

Intro: These Tofu and Vegetable Kebabs are a delightful and protein-packed option for managing insulin resistance.
Total Time: 30 minutes

Ingredients:
- 1 block extra-firm tofu, pressed and cubed
- 2 zucchinis, sliced into rounds
- 1 red bell pepper, cut into chunks
- 1 red onion, cut into chunks
- 1/4 cup low-sodium soy sauce
- 2 tablespoons olive oil
- 2 tablespoons balsamic vinegar
- 1 teaspoon dried oregano
- 1 teaspoon garlic powder
- Salt and pepper to taste
- Wooden skewers, soaked in water for 30 minutes to prevent burning

Directions:
1. In a bowl, whisk together low-sodium soy sauce, olive oil, balsamic vinegar, dried oregano, garlic powder, salt, and pepper.
2. Thread cubes of extra-firm tofu, zucchini slices, red bell pepper chunks, and red onion chunks onto the soaked wooden skewers, alternating ingredients.
3. Place the tofu and vegetable kebabs in a shallow dish and brush them with the marinade.
4. Preheat your grill to medium-high heat.
5. Grill the kebabs for about 10-12 minutes, turning occasionally, or until the tofu is lightly browned and the vegetables are tender.
6. Serve your Tofu and Vegetable Kebabs hot.
7. Enjoy these flavorful and satisfying kebabs!

Nutritional Information (per serving):
- Calories: 220
- Carbohydrates: 14g
- Protein: 14g

- Fat: 12g
- Fiber: 3g
- Sugar: 5g

Cilantro Lime Grilled Tilapia

Intro: Cilantro Lime Grilled Tilapia is a light and zesty dish that's perfect for a quick and healthy dinner, making it suitable for managing insulin resistance.
Total Time: 20 minutes

Ingredients:
- 4 tilapia fillets
- Zest and juice of 2 limes
- 2 cloves garlic, minced
- 2 tablespoons fresh cilantro, chopped
- 2 tablespoons olive oil
- Salt and pepper to taste
- Lime wedges for garnish (optional)

Directions:
1. In a bowl, combine the zest and juice of 2 limes, minced garlic, chopped fresh cilantro, olive oil, salt, and pepper. Mix well.
2. Place tilapia fillets in a shallow dish and pour the cilantro lime marinade over them. Make sure the fillets are well coated. Allow them to marinate for about 10-15 minutes.
3. Preheat your grill to medium-high heat.
4. Grill the marinated tilapia fillets for about 3-4 minutes per side, or until the fish flakes easily with a fork and is lightly browned.
5. Serve your Cilantro Lime Grilled Tilapia hot.
6. Garnish with lime wedges if desired.
7. Enjoy this zesty and refreshing dish!

Nutritional Information (per serving, excluding garnish):
- Calories: 200
- Carbohydrates: 2g
- Protein: 25g
- Fat: 10g

- Fiber: 0g
- Sugar: 0g

Quinoa-Stuffed Acorn Squash

Intro: Quinoa-Stuffed Acorn Squash is a hearty and nutritious dish that's rich in fiber and perfect for managing insulin resistance.
Total Time: 50 minutes

Ingredients:
- 2 acorn squash, halved and seeds removed
- 1 cup quinoa, rinsed and drained
- 2 cups vegetable broth
- 1 onion, diced
- 2 cloves garlic, minced
- 1 teaspoon olive oil
- 1 teaspoon dried thyme
- 1/2 cup dried cranberries
- 1/4 cup chopped pecans
- Salt and pepper to taste
- Fresh parsley leaves for garnish (optional)

Directions:
1. Preheat your oven to 375°F (190°C).
2. Brush the cut sides of the acorn squash halves with olive oil and season with salt and pepper.
3. Place the acorn squash halves cut-side down on a baking sheet lined with parchment paper.
4. Roast in the preheated oven for about 30-35 minutes, or until the squash is tender when pierced with a fork.
5. While the squash is roasting, prepare the quinoa. In a saucepan, heat olive oil over medium heat. Add diced onion and sauté for about 2-3 minutes until the onion becomes translucent.
6. Add minced garlic and dried thyme to the saucepan. Cook for another 2 minutes to toast the spices.
7. Stir in rinsed and drained quinoa. Cook for 1-2 minutes, stirring occasionally.

8. Pour in vegetable broth and bring the mixture to a boil. Reduce the heat to low, cover, and simmer for about 15-20 minutes, or until the quinoa is cooked and the liquid is absorbed.
9. Once the quinoa is done, fluff it with a fork and stir in dried cranberries and chopped pecans. Season with salt and pepper to taste.
10. Fill each roasted acorn squash half with the quinoa mixture.
11. Return the stuffed acorn squash halves to the oven and bake for an additional 10 minutes to heat through.
12. Garnish with fresh parsley leaves if desired.
13. Serve your Quinoa-Stuffed Acorn Squash hot.
14. Enjoy this comforting and nutritious meal!

Nutritional Information (per serving, excluding garnish):
- Calories: 300
- Carbohydrates: 60g
- Protein: 7g
- Fat: 6g
- Fiber: 10g
- Sugar: 12g

Portobello Mushroom and Spinach Lasagna

Intro: Portobello Mushroom and Spinach Lasagna is a savory and satisfying dish that's packed with flavor, making it suitable for managing insulin resistance.
Total Time: 1 hour 15 minutes
Ingredients:
- 9 lasagna noodles, cooked and drained
- 4 large portobello mushrooms, sliced
- 4 cups fresh spinach leaves
- 2 cups ricotta cheese
- 2 cups shredded mozzarella cheese
- 1/2 cup grated Parmesan cheese
- 2 cloves garlic, minced
- 1 egg
- 2 cups marinara sauce (store-bought or homemade)
- 1 teaspoon dried basil
- Salt and pepper to taste

- Fresh basil leaves for garnish (optional)

Directions:

1. Preheat your oven to 375°F (190°C).
2. In a large skillet, sauté sliced portobello mushrooms over medium heat for about 5-7 minutes, or until they release their moisture and become tender. Remove from the skillet and set aside.
3. In the same skillet, add fresh spinach leaves and sauté for about 2-3 minutes until they wilt. Remove from heat and set aside.
4. In a bowl, combine ricotta cheese, 1 cup shredded mozzarella cheese, grated Parmesan cheese, minced garlic, egg, dried basil, salt, and pepper. Mix well.
5. In a 9x13-inch baking dish, spread a thin layer of marinara sauce on the bottom.
6. Place 3 cooked lasagna noodles on top of the sauce.
7. Spread half of the ricotta cheese mixture over the noodles.
8. Layer half of the sautéed mushrooms and half of the wilted spinach on top of the ricotta mixture.
9. Repeat the layers: 3 lasagna noodles, remaining ricotta cheese mixture, remaining sautéed mushrooms, remaining wilted spinach.
10. Top with the remaining 3 lasagna noodles and the remaining marinara sauce.
11. Sprinkle the remaining 1 cup of shredded mozzarella cheese on top.
12. Cover the baking dish with aluminum foil.
13. Bake in the preheated oven for about 25-30 minutes, or until the lasagna is hot and bubbly.
14. Remove the foil and bake for an additional 5-10 minutes, or until the cheese is golden brown.
15. Garnish with fresh basil leaves if desired.
16. Serve your Portobello Mushroom and Spinach Lasagna hot.
17. Enjoy this flavorful and comforting lasagna!

Nutritional Information (per serving, excluding garnish):

- Calories: 350
- Carbohydrates: 30g
- Protein: 20g
- Fat: 16g
- Fiber: 4g

- Sugar: 4g

Baked Sweet Potato with Black Bean Chili

Intro: Baked Sweet Potato with Black Bean Chili is a hearty and nutritious meal that's perfect for managing insulin resistance.
Total Time: 1 hour

Ingredients:
- 4 medium sweet potatoes
- 1 can (15 ounces) black beans, drained and rinsed
- 1 can (14 ounces) diced tomatoes
- 1 onion, chopped
- 2 cloves garlic, minced
- 1 tablespoon olive oil
- 1 tablespoon chili powder
- 1 teaspoon ground cumin
- Salt and pepper to taste
- Chopped fresh cilantro for garnish (optional)
- Greek yogurt or sour cream for topping (optional)

Directions:
1. Preheat your oven to 400°F (200°C).
2. Scrub the sweet potatoes and pierce them with a fork.
3. Place the sweet potatoes on a baking sheet and bake in the preheated oven for about 45-50 minutes, or until they are tender when pierced with a fork.
4. While the sweet potatoes are baking, prepare the black bean chili. In a large skillet, heat olive oil over medium heat. Add chopped onion and sauté for about 2-3 minutes until the onion becomes translucent.
5. Add minced garlic, chili powder, and ground cumin to the skillet. Cook for another 2 minutes to toast the spices.
6. Stir in diced tomatoes (with their juice) and drained black beans. Simmer for about 10-15 minutes, or until the chili thickens and the flavors meld together. Season with salt and pepper to taste.
7. Once the sweet potatoes are done, remove them from the oven and let them cool slightly.
8. Slice each sweet potato in half lengthwise and fluff the flesh with a fork.

9. Top each sweet potato half with a generous spoonful of black bean chili.
10. Garnish with chopped fresh cilantro and a dollop of Greek yogurt or sour cream if desired.
11. Serve your Baked Sweet Potato with Black Bean Chili hot.
12. Enjoy this hearty and satisfying meal!

Nutritional Information (per serving, excluding garnishes):
- Calories: 300
- Carbohydrates: 60g
- Protein: 10g
- Fat: 3g
- Fiber: 10g
- Sugar: 10g

Ratatouille Stuffed Bell Peppers

Intro: Ratatouille Stuffed Bell Peppers are a delicious and vegetable-packed dish that's perfect for managing insulin resistance.
Total Time: 50 minutes

Ingredients:
- 4 large bell peppers, any color
- 2 zucchinis, diced
- 1 eggplant, diced
- 1 onion, diced
- 2 cloves garlic, minced
- 1 can (14 ounces) diced tomatoes
- 2 tablespoons olive oil
- 1 teaspoon dried thyme
- 1/2 cup shredded mozzarella cheese
- Fresh basil leaves for garnish (optional)
- Salt and pepper to taste

Directions:
1. Preheat your oven to 375°F (190°C).
2. Cut the tops off the bell peppers and remove the seeds and membranes. Set aside.

3. In a large skillet, heat olive oil over medium heat. Add diced onion and sauté for about 2-3 minutes until the onion becomes translucent.
4. Add minced garlic, diced zucchini, and diced eggplant to the skillet. Sauté for about 5-7 minutes until the vegetables are softened.
5. Stir in diced tomatoes (with their juice), dried thyme, salt, and pepper. Cook for another 2-3 minutes to heat through.
6. Spoon the ratatouille mixture into the hollowed-out bell peppers, packing it down firmly.
7. Place the stuffed bell peppers in a baking dish.
8. Sprinkle shredded mozzarella cheese on top of each stuffed bell pepper.
9. Cover the baking dish with aluminum foil.
10. Bake in the preheated oven for about 25-30 minutes, or until the bell peppers are tender and the cheese is melted and bubbly.
11. Garnish with fresh basil leaves if desired.
12. Serve your Ratatouille Stuffed Bell Peppers hot.
13. Enjoy this flavorful and vegetable-filled dish!

Nutritional Information (per stuffed bell pepper, excluding garnish):
- Calories: 200
- Carbohydrates: 25g
- Protein: 8g
- Fat: 8g
- Fiber: 7g
- Sugar: 10g

Teriyaki Pork Tenderloin with Broccoli

Intro: Teriyaki Pork Tenderloin with Broccoli is a flavorful and protein-rich dish that's suitable for managing insulin resistance.
Total Time: 30 minutes

Ingredients:
- 2 pork tenderloins
- 1 cup low-sodium teriyaki sauce
- 1 tablespoon olive oil
- 2 cups broccoli florets
- 2 cloves garlic, minced

- 1 teaspoon fresh ginger, minced
- Sesame seeds for garnish (optional)
- Sliced green onions for garnish (optional)

Directions:

1. In a bowl, marinate pork tenderloins in low-sodium teriyaki sauce for about 10-15 minutes.
2. Preheat your grill to medium-high heat.
3. Remove pork tenderloins from the marinade and grill for about 15-20 minutes, turning occasionally, or until they are cooked through and have grill marks. The internal temperature should reach 145°F (63°C).
4. While the pork is grilling, heat olive oil in a large skillet over medium-high heat.
5. Add minced garlic and minced fresh ginger to the skillet. Sauté for about 1-2 minutes until fragrant.
6. Add broccoli florets to the skillet and stir-fry for about 3-4 minutes until they are tender-crisp.
7. Once the pork tenderloins are done grilling, let them rest for a few minutes before slicing them.
8. Serve sliced pork tenderloins over stir-fried broccoli.
9. Garnish with sesame seeds and sliced green onions if desired.
10. Enjoy this flavorful and savory dish!

Nutritional Information (per serving, excluding garnishes):

- Calories: 300
- Carbohydrates: 10g
- Protein: 30g
- Fat: 10g
- Fiber: 2g
- Sugar: 6g

Thai Red Curry with Tofu

Intro: Thai Red Curry with Tofu is a spicy and flavorful dish that's suitable for managing insulin resistance.
Total Time: 30 minutes

Ingredients:

- 1 block extra-firm tofu, cubed
- 1 can (14 ounces) coconut milk
- 2 tablespoons red curry paste
- 2 cups mixed vegetables (bell peppers, broccoli, carrots, etc.)
- 1 tablespoon soy sauce or tamari
- 1 tablespoon brown sugar or coconut sugar
- 2 tablespoons fresh basil leaves, chopped
- Cooked brown rice for serving

Directions:

1. In a large skillet or wok, heat a small amount of oil over medium-high heat.
2. Add cubed extra-firm tofu to the skillet and stir-fry for about 5-7 minutes until it's lightly browned and slightly crispy. Remove the tofu from the skillet and set aside.
3. In the same skillet, add red curry paste and sauté for about 1-2 minutes to release its aroma.
4. Pour in coconut milk and stir to combine with the curry paste.
5. Add mixed vegetables to the skillet and simmer for about 10 minutes, or until the vegetables are tender.
6. Stir in soy sauce (or tamari) and brown sugar (or coconut sugar).
7. Return the cooked tofu to the skillet and stir to coat it with the curry sauce.
8. Add chopped fresh basil leaves and cook for an additional 2 minutes.
9. Serve your Thai Red Curry with Tofu hot over cooked brown rice.
10. Enjoy this spicy and aromatic curry!

Nutritional Information (per serving):

- Calories: 400
- Carbohydrates: 20g
- Protein: 15g
- Fat: 30g
- Fiber: 4g
- Sugar: 6g

Mediterranean Baked Cod

Intro: Mediterranean Baked Cod is a flavorful and heart-healthy dish that's perfect for managing insulin resistance.

Total Time: 25 minutes

Ingredients:
- 4 cod fillets
- 1 can (14 ounces) diced tomatoes, drained
- 1/2 cup Kalamata olives, pitted and sliced
- 1/4 cup fresh parsley leaves, chopped
- 2 cloves garlic, minced
- 1 teaspoon dried oregano
- 1/4 cup crumbled feta cheese (optional)
- Lemon wedges for garnish (optional)
- Salt and pepper to taste

Directions:
1. Preheat your oven to 375°F (190°C).
2. In a bowl, combine drained diced tomatoes, sliced Kalamata olives, chopped fresh parsley leaves, minced garlic, and dried oregano. Mix well.
3. Season cod fillets with salt and pepper.
4. Place the cod fillets in a baking dish.
5. Spoon the tomato and olive mixture over the cod fillets.
6. If desired, sprinkle crumbled feta cheese on top of the cod fillets.
7. Cover the baking dish with aluminum foil.
8. Bake in the preheated oven for about 15-20 minutes, or until the cod flakes easily with a fork and is opaque.
9. Garnish with lemon wedges if desired.
10. Serve your Mediterranean Baked Cod hot.
11. Enjoy this Mediterranean-inspired dish!

Nutritional Information (per serving, excluding garnishes and optional feta):
- Calories: 200
- Carbohydrates: 5g
- Protein: 30g

- Fat: 6g
- Fiber: 2g
- Sugar: 2g

Roasted Veggie and Chickpea Bowl

Intro: Roasted Veggie and Chickpea Bowl is a nutritious and satisfying dish that's perfect for managing insulin resistance.
Total Time: 40 minutes

Ingredients:
- 2 cups cauliflower florets
- 2 cups broccoli florets
- 1 can (15 ounces) chickpeas, drained and rinsed
- 2 tablespoons olive oil
- 1 teaspoon smoked paprika
- 1 teaspoon garlic powder
- 1 teaspoon ground cumin
- Salt and pepper to taste
- 2 cups cooked quinoa
- 1/4 cup tahini dressing
- Chopped fresh parsley for garnish (optional)
- Lemon wedges for garnish (optional)

Directions:
1. Preheat your oven to 425°F (220°C).
2. In a large mixing bowl, combine cauliflower florets, broccoli florets, and drained and rinsed chickpeas.
3. Drizzle olive oil over the vegetables and chickpeas. Sprinkle smoked paprika, garlic powder, ground cumin, salt, and pepper. Toss everything together to coat evenly.
4. Spread the vegetable and chickpea mixture in a single layer on a baking sheet lined with parchment paper.
5. Roast in the preheated oven for about 20-25 minutes, or until the vegetables are tender and slightly crispy.
6. While the vegetables are roasting, prepare quinoa according to package instructions.

7. Divide cooked quinoa among serving bowls.
8. Top with the roasted vegetable and chickpea mixture.
9. Drizzle tahini dressing over the bowl.
10. Garnish with chopped fresh parsley and lemon wedges if desired.
11. Serve your Roasted Veggie and Chickpea Bowl hot.
12. Enjoy this nutritious and flavorful bowl!

Nutritional Information (per serving, excluding garnishes):
- Calories: 400
- Carbohydrates: 50g
- Protein: 12g
- Fat: 18g
- Fiber: 9g
- Sugar: 5g

Lemon Dill Grilled Swordfish

Intro: Lemon Dill Grilled Swordfish is a light and flavorful dish that's perfect for managing insulin resistance.
Total Time: 20 minutes

Ingredients:
- 4 swordfish steaks
- Zest and juice of 1 lemon
- 2 tablespoons fresh dill, chopped
- 2 cloves garlic, minced
- 2 tablespoons olive oil
- Salt and pepper to taste
- Lemon wedges for garnish (optional)
- Fresh dill sprigs for garnish (optional)

Directions:
1. In a bowl, combine the zest and juice of 1 lemon, chopped fresh dill, minced garlic, olive oil, salt, and pepper. Mix well.
2. Place swordfish steaks in a shallow dish and pour the lemon dill marinade over them. Make sure the steaks are well coated. Allow them to marinate for about 10-15 minutes.

3. Preheat your grill to medium-high heat.
4. Grill the marinated swordfish steaks for about 3-4 minutes per side, or until the fish is cooked through and has grill marks. The internal temperature should reach 145°F (63°C).
5. Serve your Lemon Dill Grilled Swordfish hot.
6. Garnish with lemon wedges and fresh dill sprigs if desired.
7. Enjoy this light and zesty dish!

Nutritional Information (per serving, excluding garnishes):
- Calories: 250
- Carbohydrates: 1g
- Protein: 30g
- Fat: 13g
- Fiber: 0g
- Sugar: 0g

Made in United States
North Haven, CT
11 January 2024

47334032R00041